BLANK
COMIC BOOK

135 PAGES

8.5 X 11 IN / 21.59 X 27.94 CM

DRAW YOUR OWN COMICS

For more cool books, please visit:

www.ArnieLightning.com/books

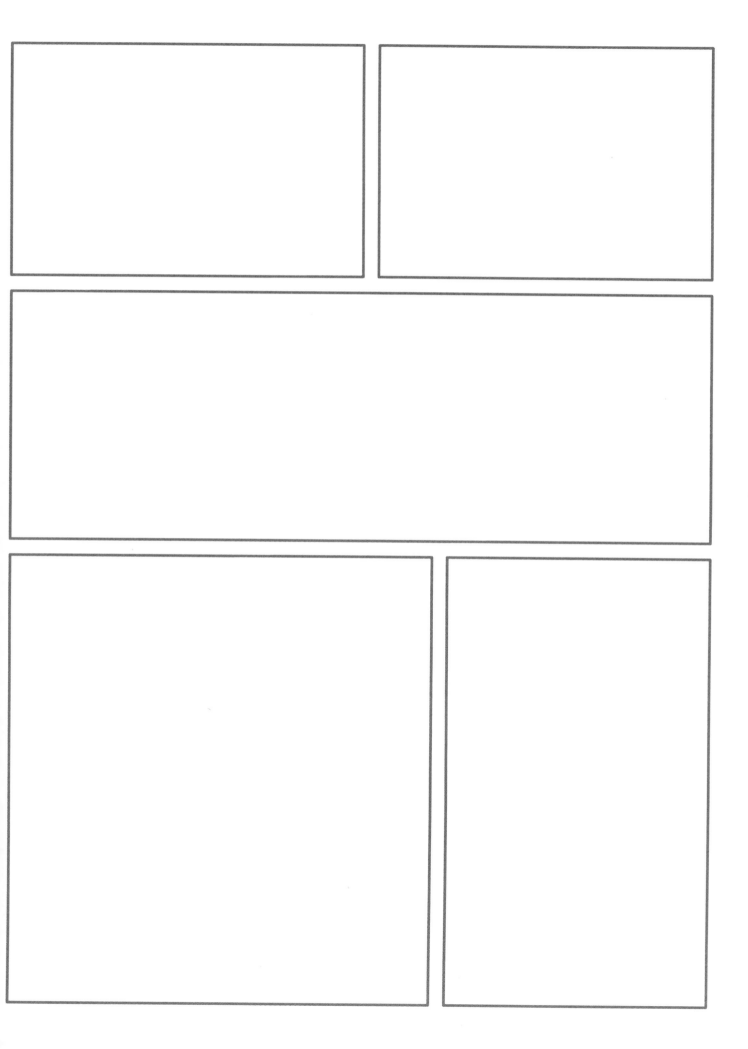

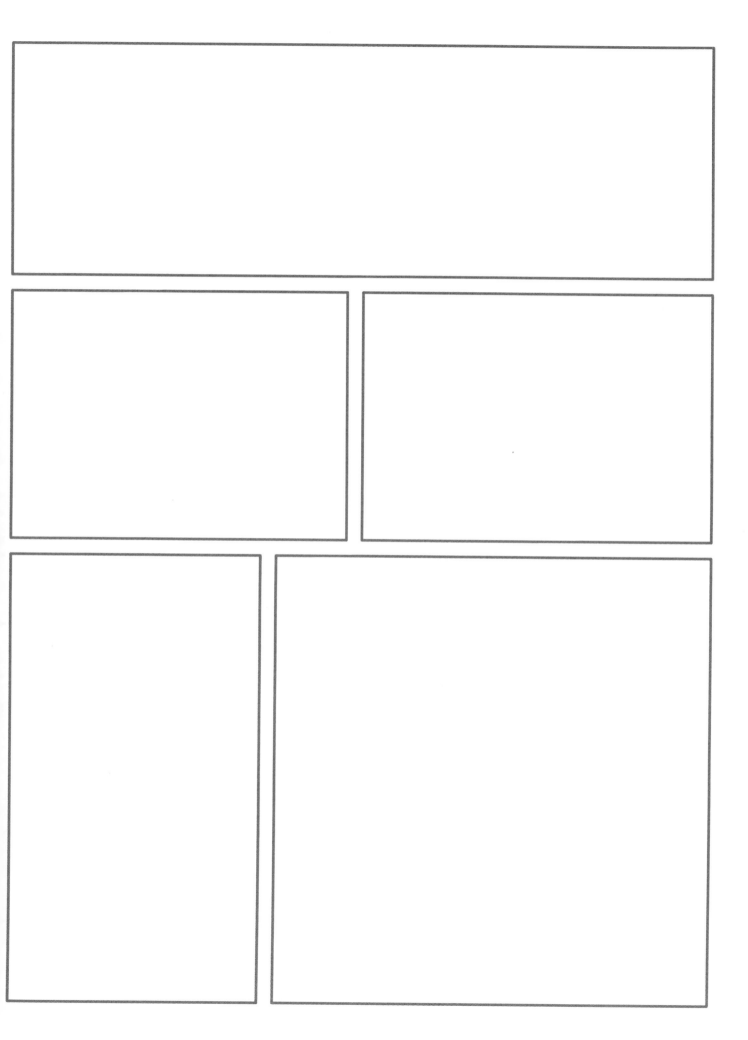

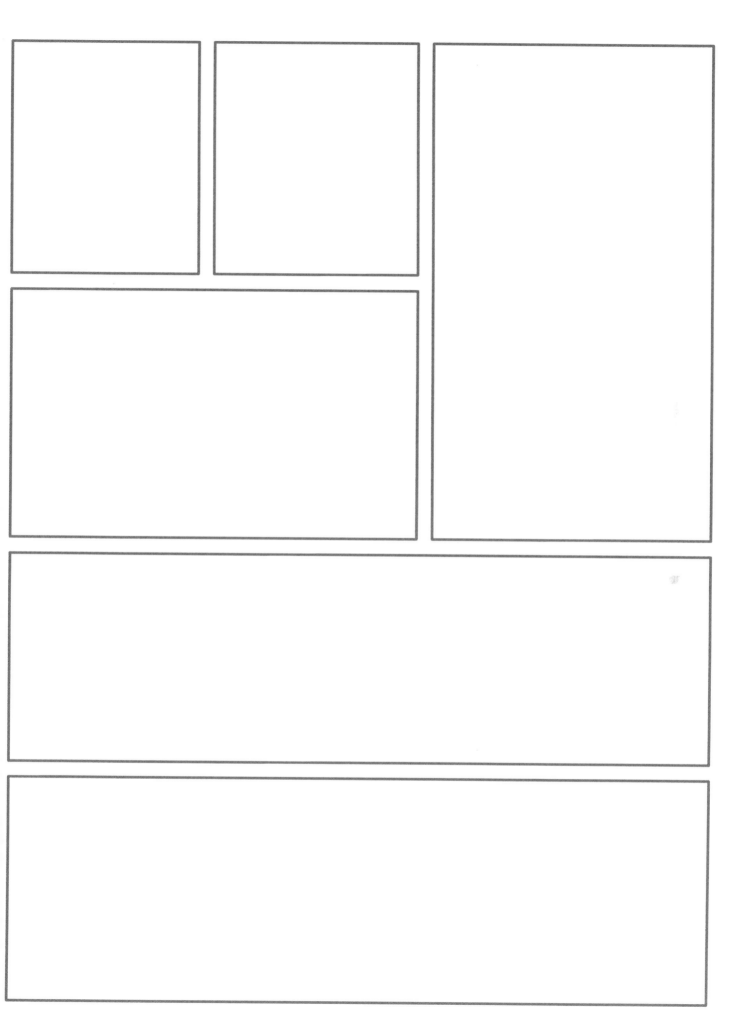

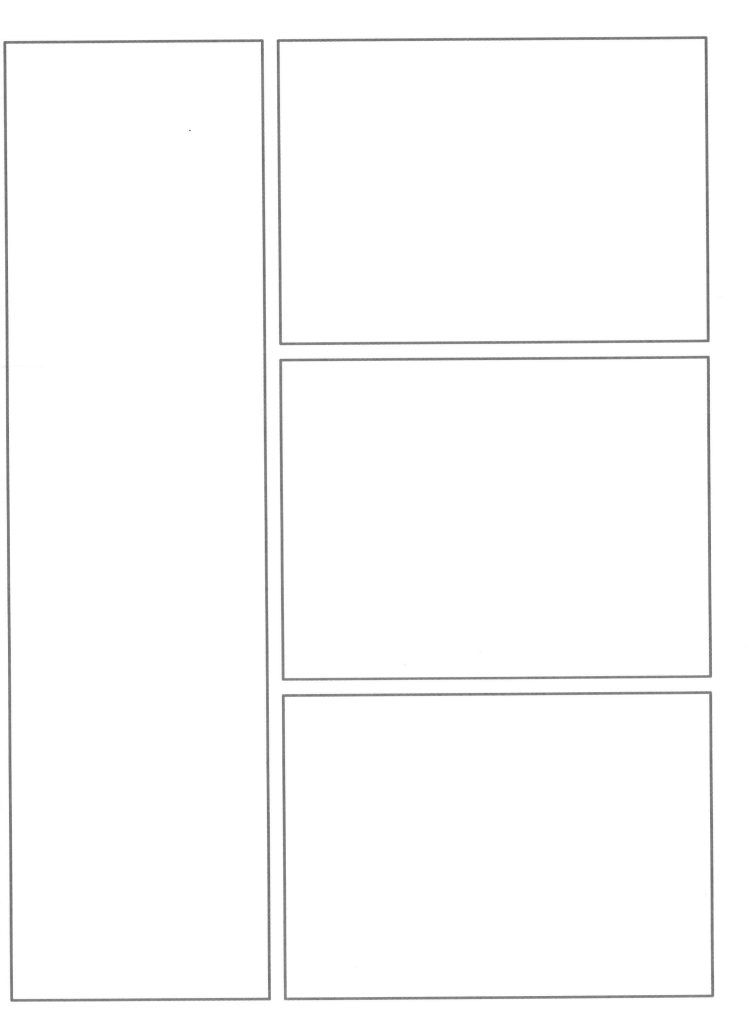

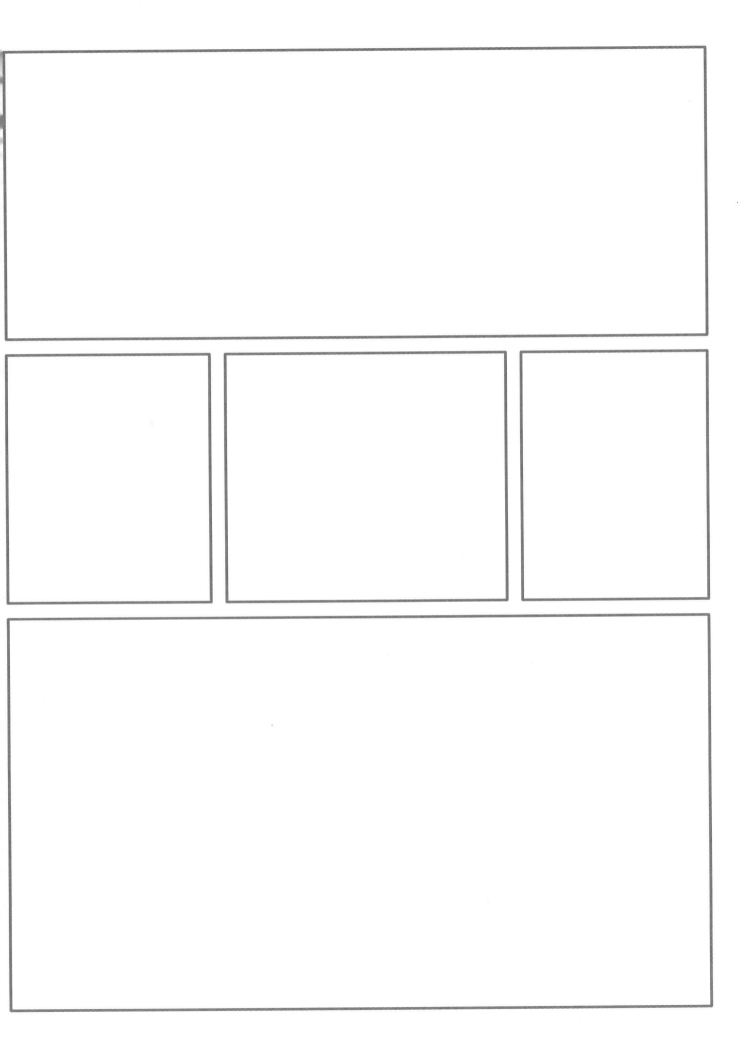

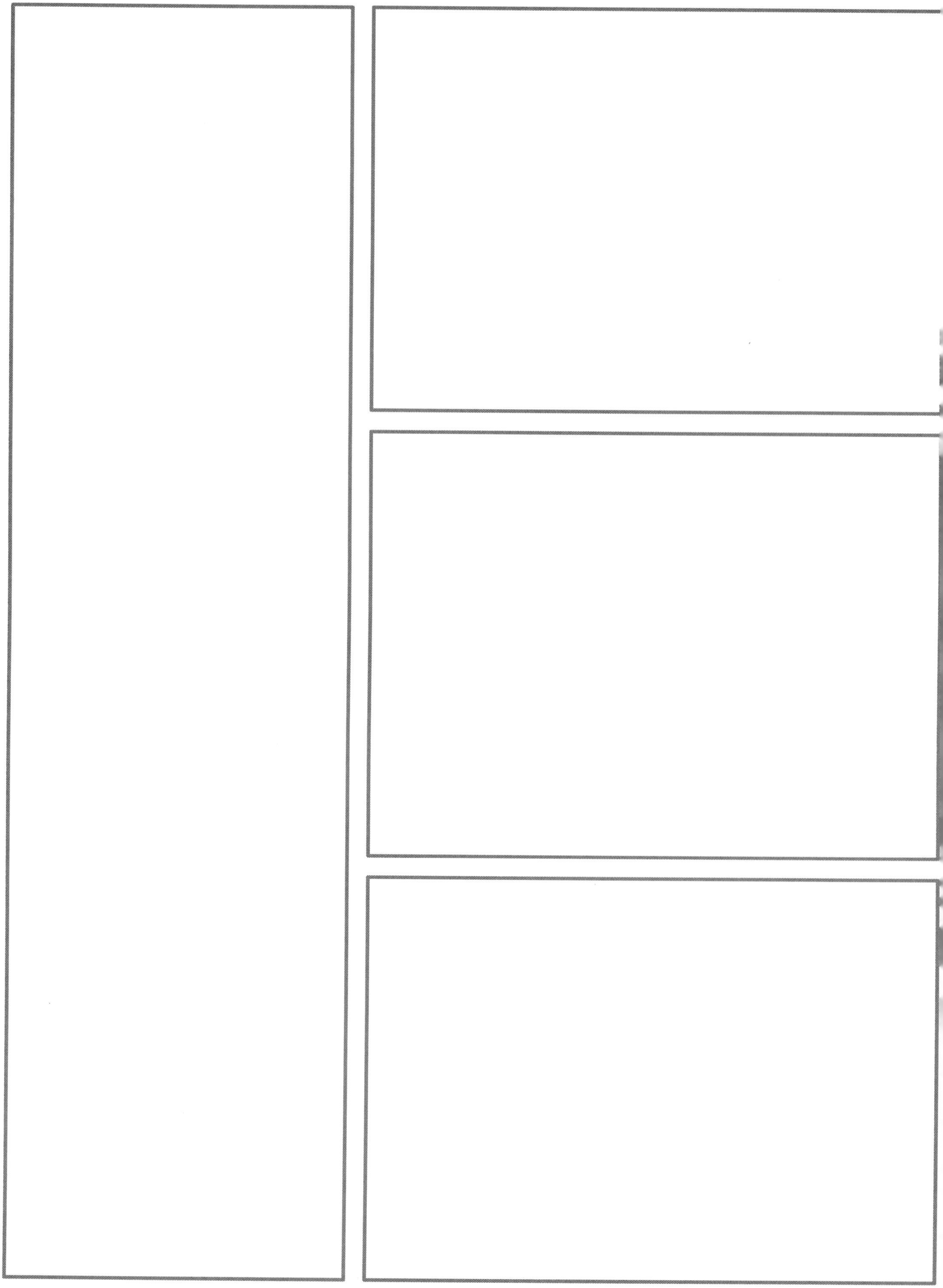

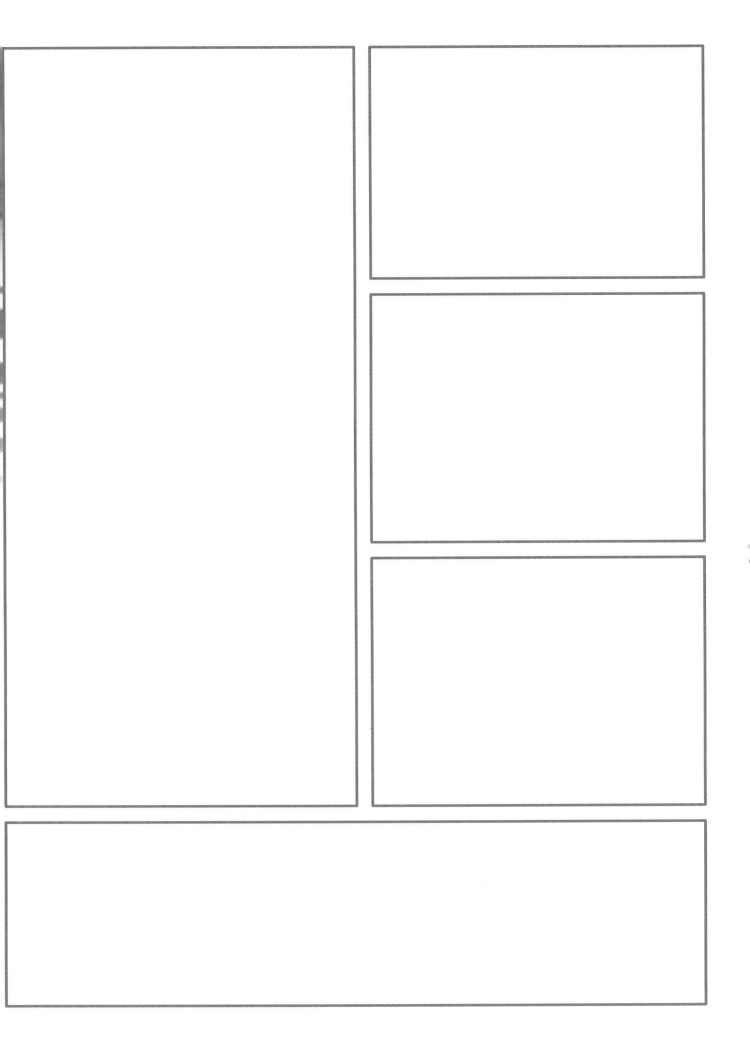

Printed in Great Britain
by Amazon

51478670R00079